Jean Expressions

By Lisa Katz

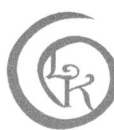

Published by Lisa Katz, Gainesville, Florida.

Printed in the United States of America.
Book design: **Chermont Design**. Photos by Dominique Attaway.

ISBN-13: 978-1480147577
ISBN-10: 1480147575

First Edition

This book is dedicated to all my girlfriends
that have both contributed quotes as well as
laughed along the way as I gathered them.
A big thank you to all of my friends
that allowed their beautiful bodies to be
photographed by Dominique Attaway.
She came to a private party hosted at the Jean Theory,
a chic store in downtown Charlottesville, Virginia,
where we laughed as if we were
at a sleepover with 25 friends!

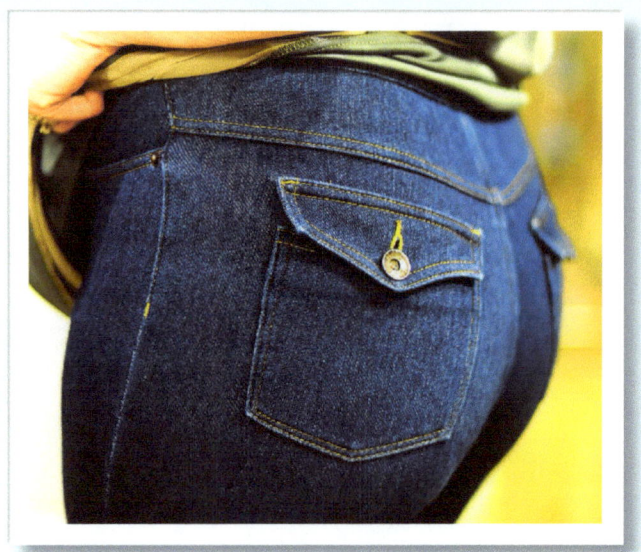

Some of the most common pieces of clothing in a wardrobe for people nowadays are jeans. The versatility and ease of wearing them is immeasurable. You can dress them up with heels or boots or be more casual with sneakers or flip-flops. Either way, as far as I am concerned, they are impossible to do without. They are an essential part of my wardrobe and have been since I was a child. When I was growing up, jeans were also called dungarees (but let's not go there!). Jeans come in all styles: boot-cut, flare-bottoms, straight-leg, skinny and the ever-popular low-rise jean. Let's take a minute to review this last concept. The low-rise jean has taken over the shelves of popular clothing stores everywhere! Clearly, someone very thin with no hips (and probably never had any children) designed this style. It works for teenagers, models, the occasional woman and the occasional man. More often than not, however, the low-rise jean has made shopping for the perfect jean the perfect nightmare! In fact, I recently decided it was time to update my jean wardrobe. Just so you know, people do have a jean wardrobe these days. Well, the comments I was making in the dressing room started me thinking about the comments other women (and men) are making while going through the same torture.

And it IS torturous! It was these comments that sparked me to create this book. Women like to commiserate with other women about their shopping experiences. I write 'women' because I am not sure if men even make a grunt, let alone a comment, when trying on clothing in a dressing room. In fact, do most men even use a dressing room? I decided to write this book to show women that, while looking for the perfect pair of jeans, they are not alone in their thoughts. I mean, is there a good pair of jeans for every type of body? Even more important, why are women so incredibly hard on themselves? Women just need to embrace themselves in all their glory. That leads me back to women sharing with other women.

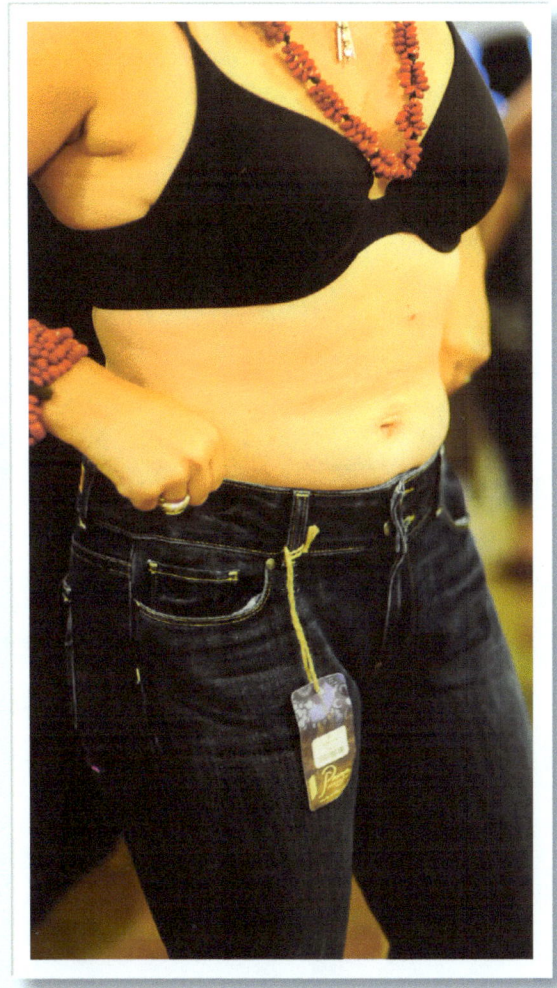

Comments made in the dressing rooms should be available for all to hear. We are not alone in our thoughts. Here are some of the good ones that either I said, overheard, or friends and family have made.

Enjoy,

Lisa Katz

A good pair of jeans can
hold an awful lot of power. – M.L.

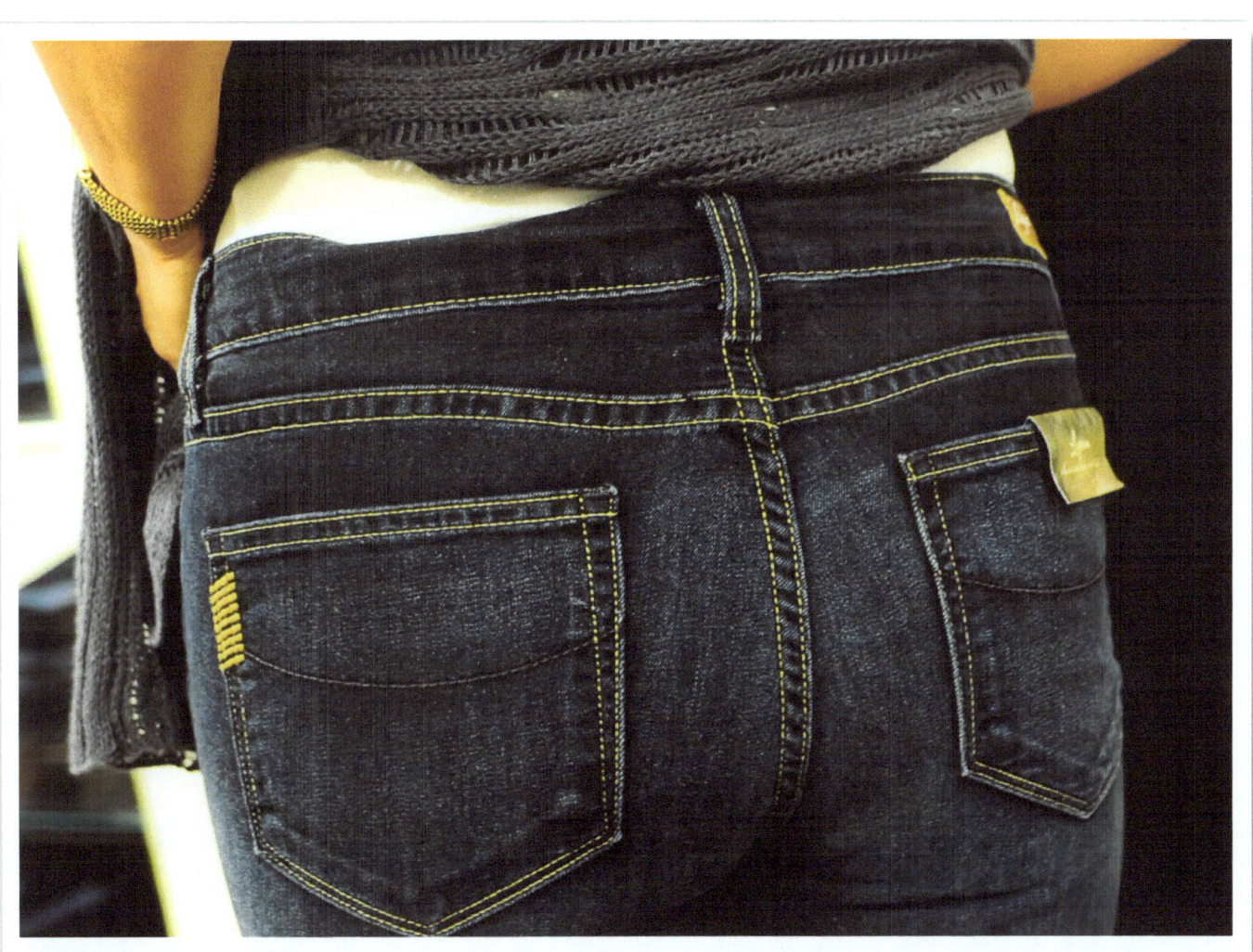

"Hey, do these jeans make me look fat?".
Boyfriend's response: "No, your ass makes you look fat!". – R.Z.

These jeans exacerbate the genetic betrayal that is my destiny. – K.S.

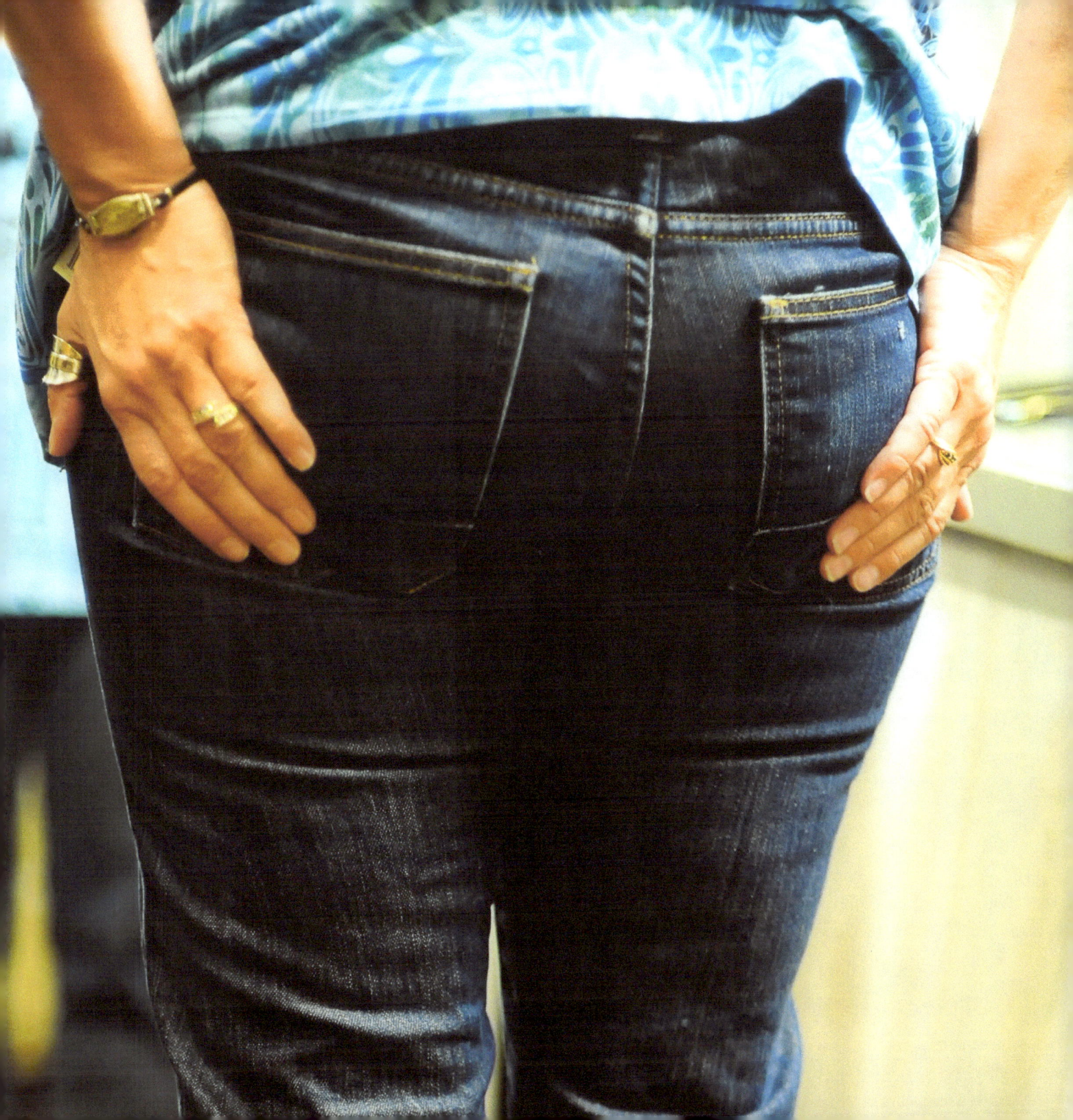

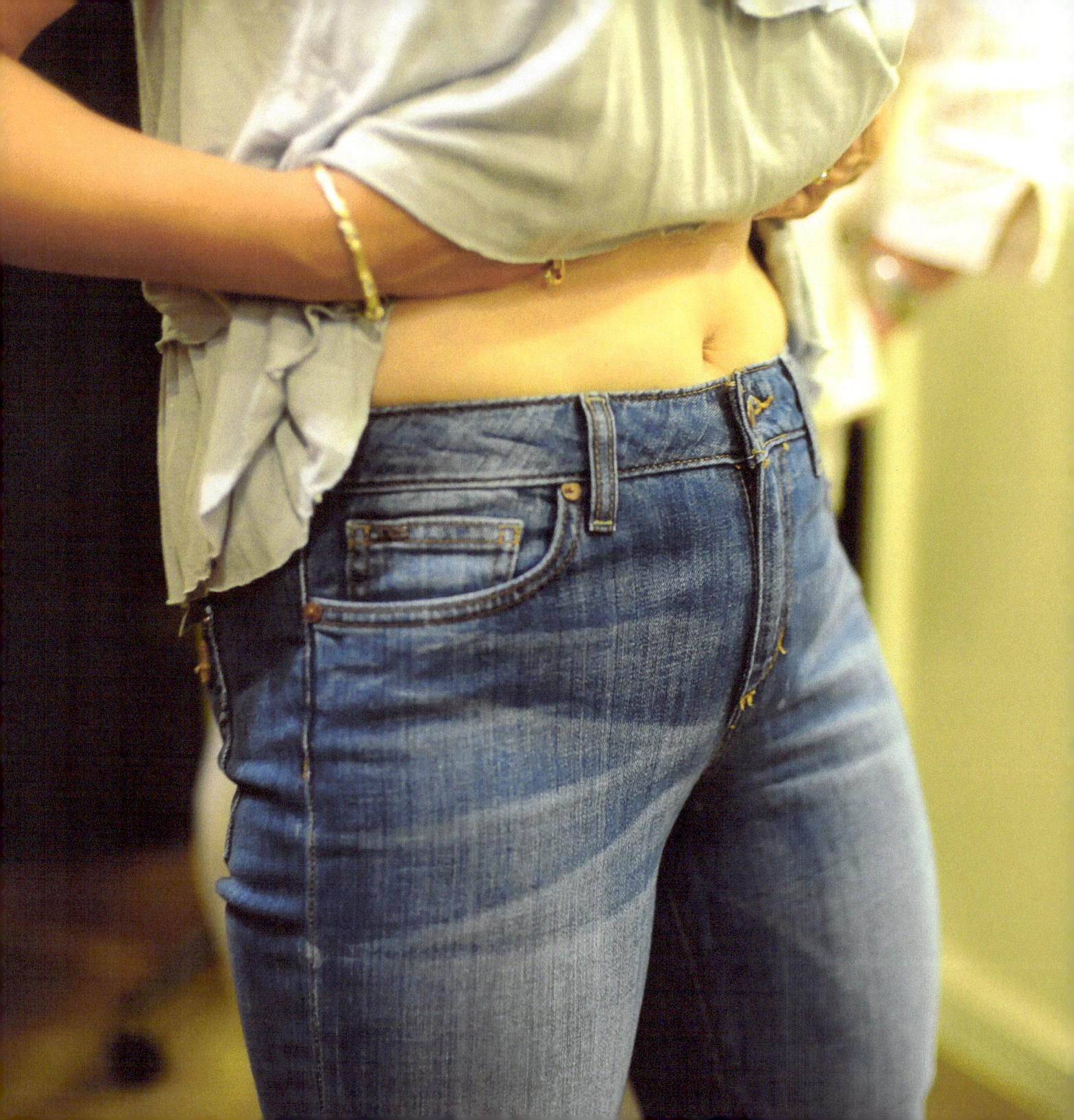

I think my muffin top is getting smaller... I have gone from a Starbucks muffin to a regular muffin! – A.S.

Why can't my butt be shaped more like an apple? If it were, these jeans would actually rock instead of roll. – R.M.

I could tell you that those look good on you but then I would feel bad the rest of the day. – Overheard

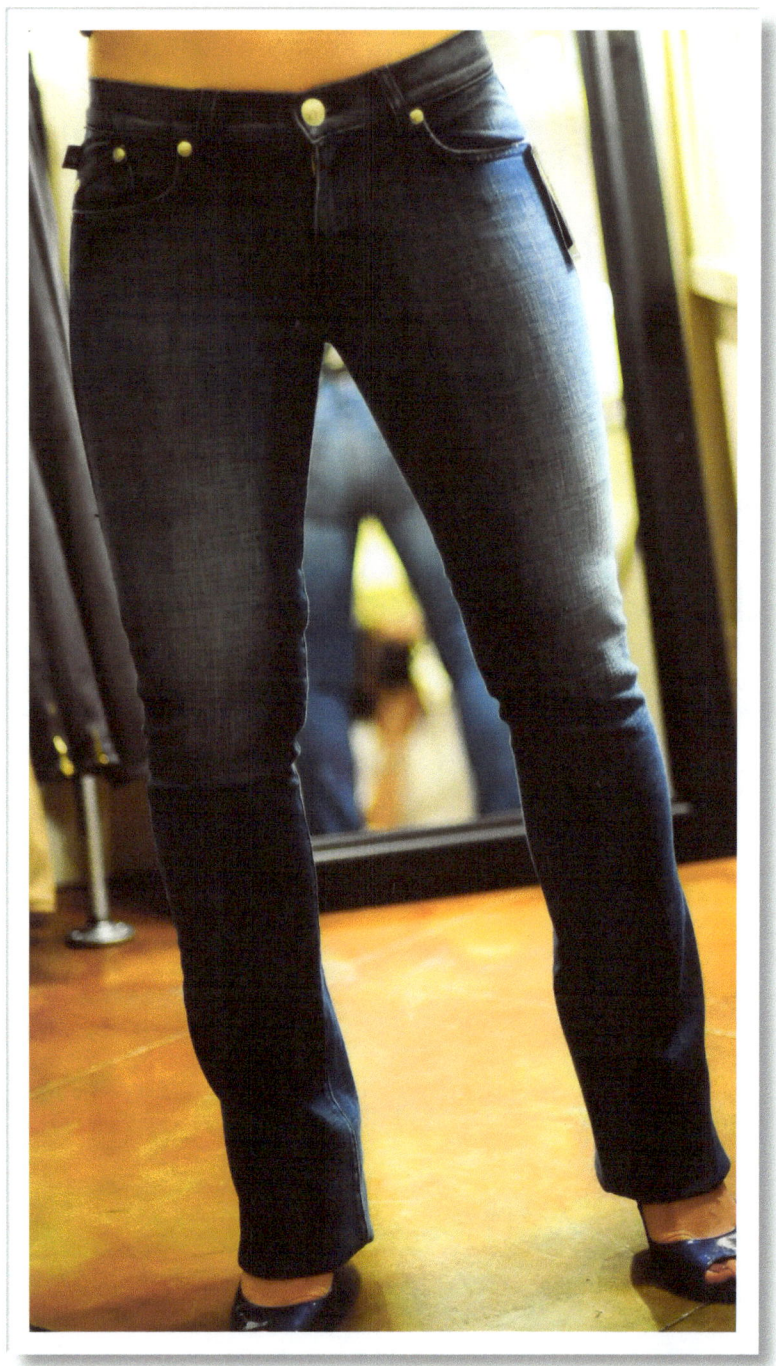

My jeans are so tight that even an army of men couldn't get them off. – S.N.

When I sat down, the whole muffin showed. – S.K.

I have to go get my hooker shoes. Just having them on makes my jeans look amazing! – H.A.

Are you freaking kidding me? These jeans should be banned! – Overheard

They hug your ass and make you look perky. – J.K.

Maybe I'm too old to wear skinny jeans. – A.C.

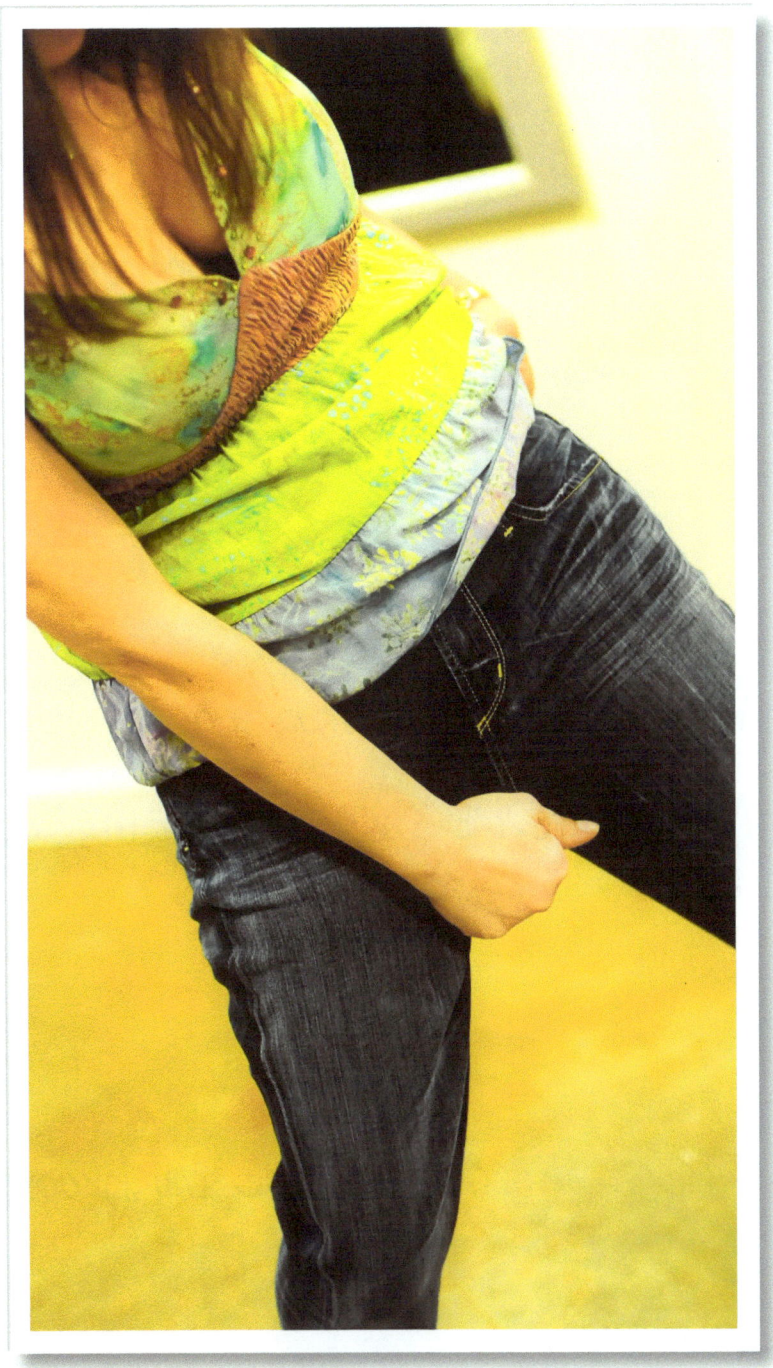

I need a fabulous pair of jeans that make me look fabulous when I put them on, not like a saggy, baggy 40-year old with no shape. – A.C.

Who do they make these for... twelve-year olds? My WHOLE ass is hanging out! – A.B.

These jeans make me mushroom. – J.T.

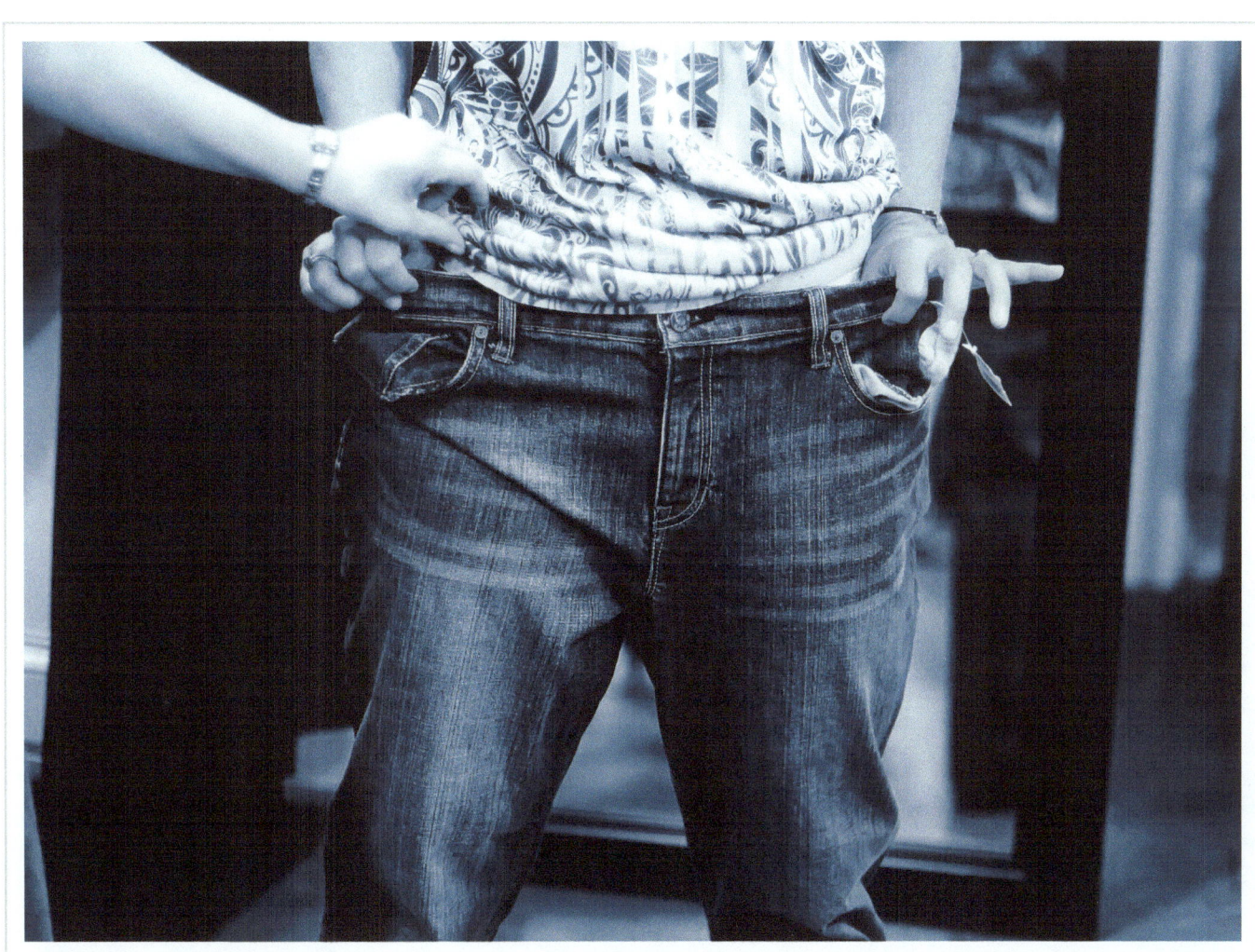

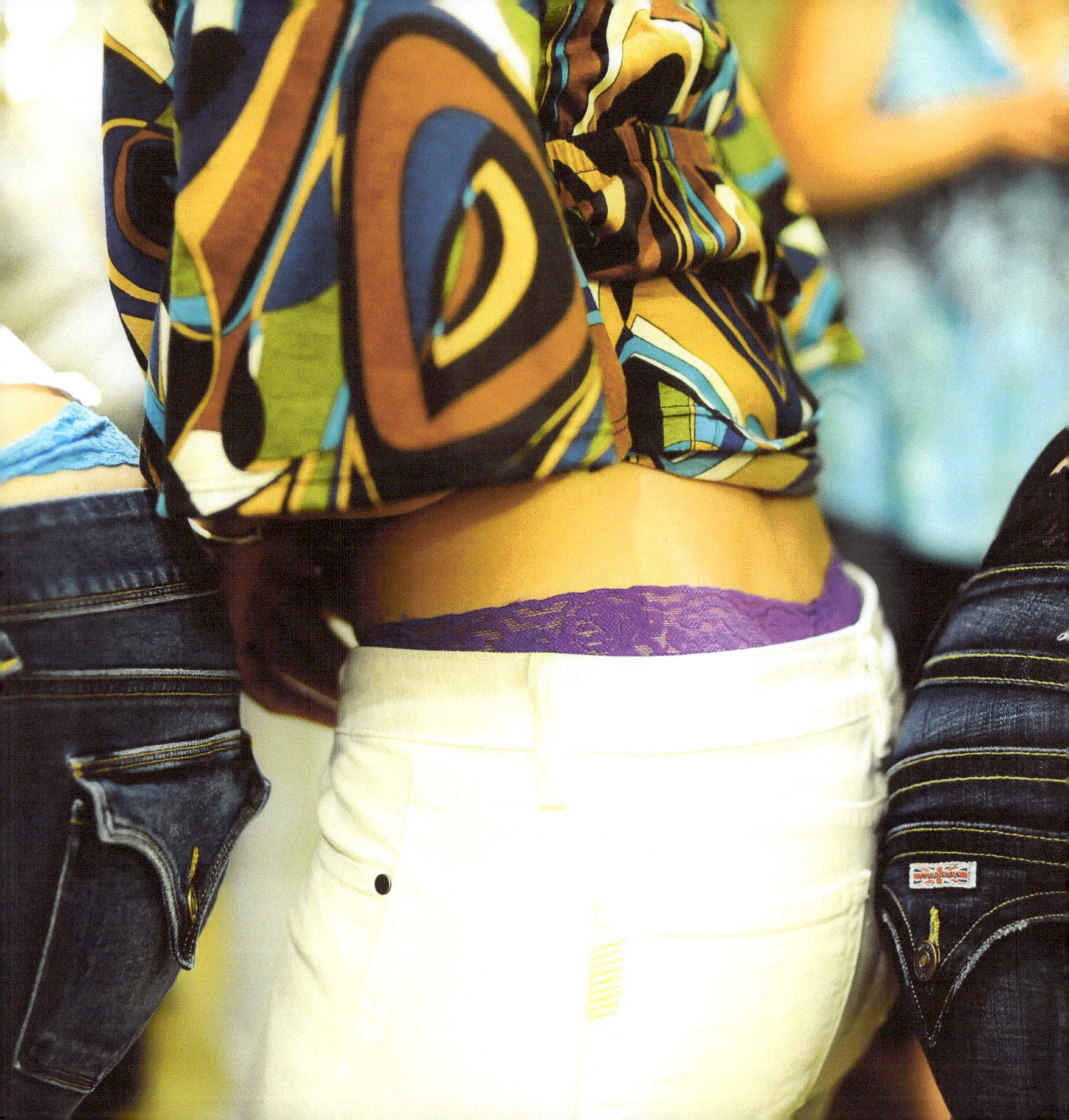

Can you see the top of my thong in these when I bend down? – A.B.

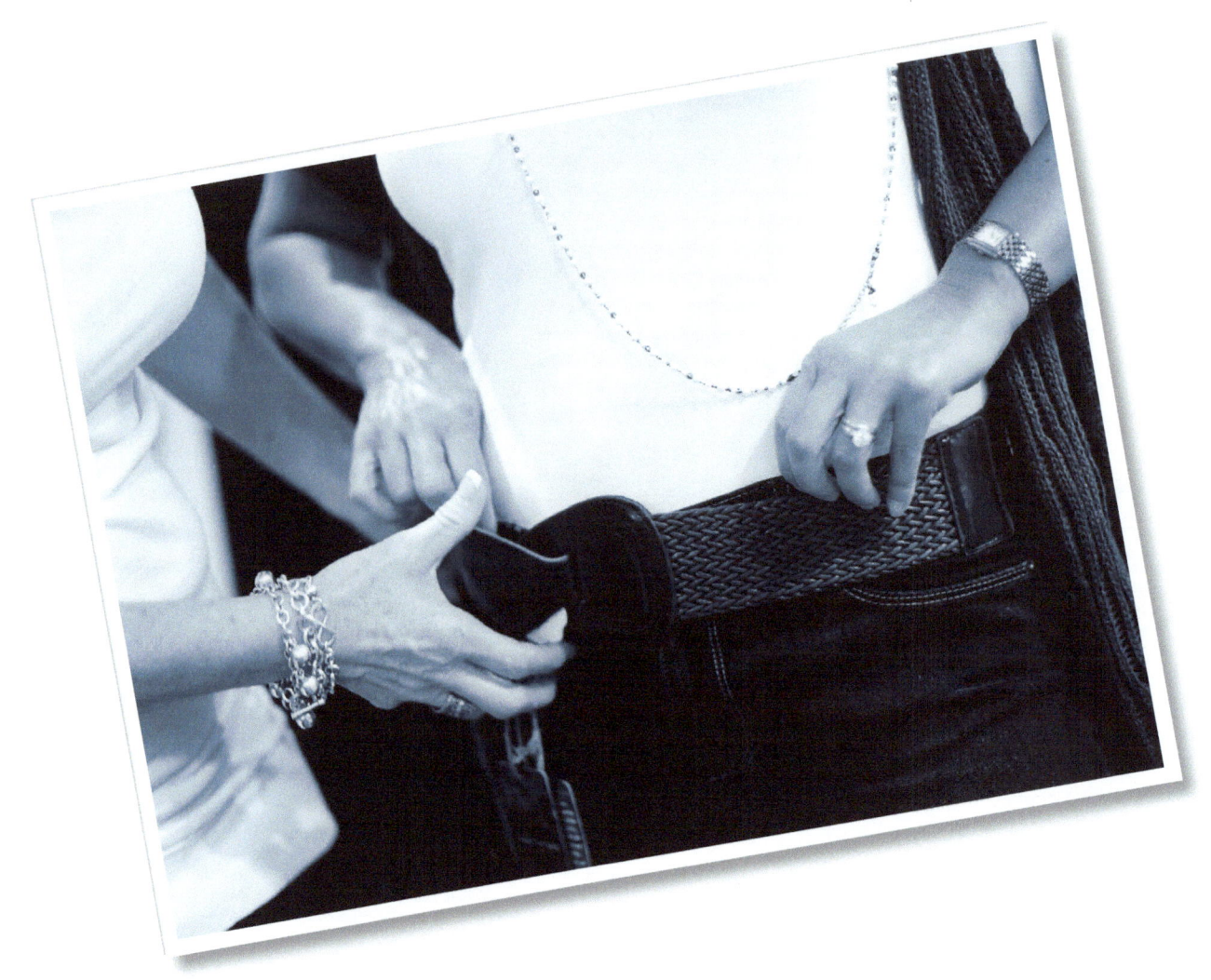

Where are the jeans from the 90's that suck in tummy fat and don't leave me with a muffin top? – J.K.

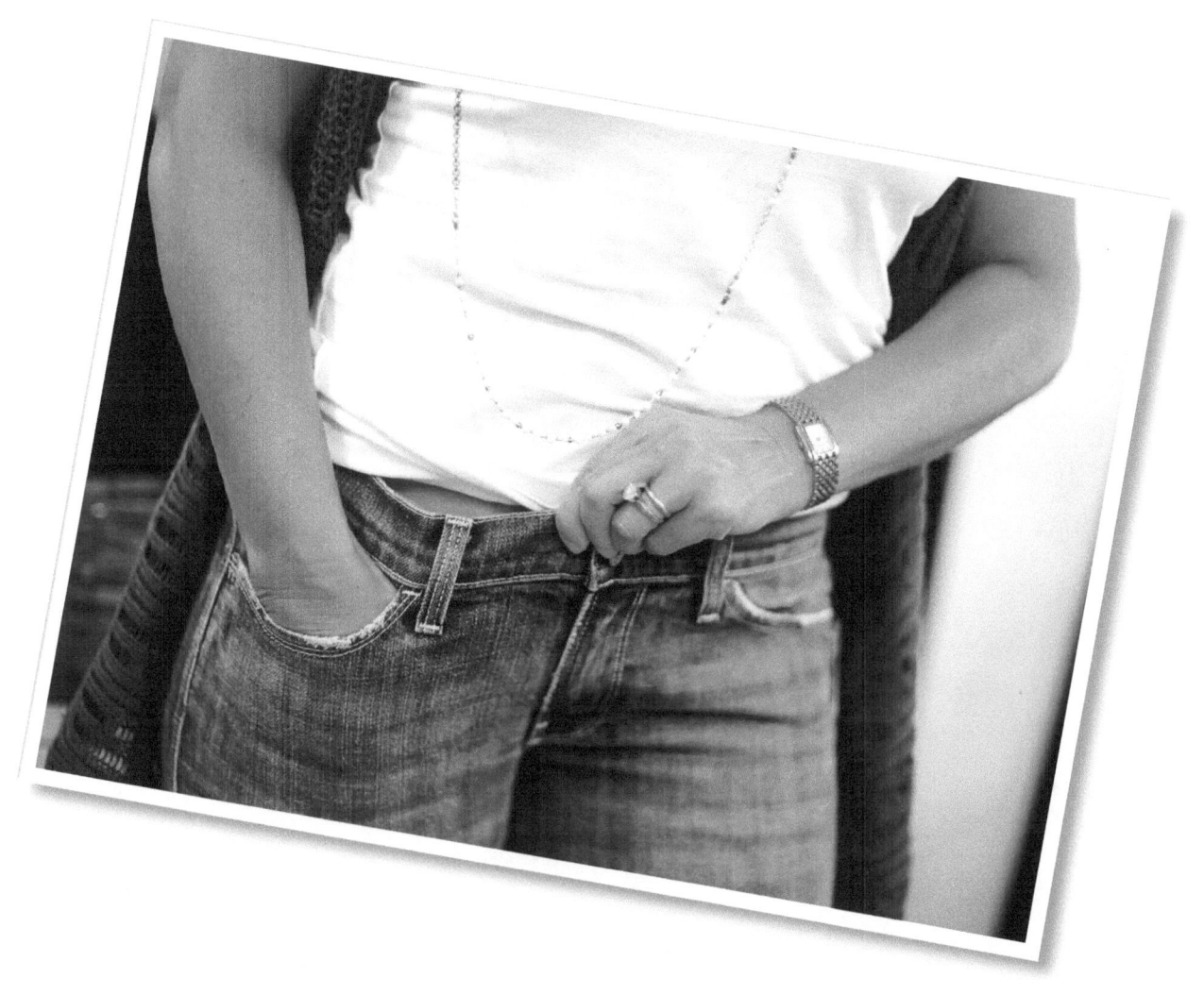

I'd have to stop eating for three weeks to be able to squeeze into these! – Overheard.

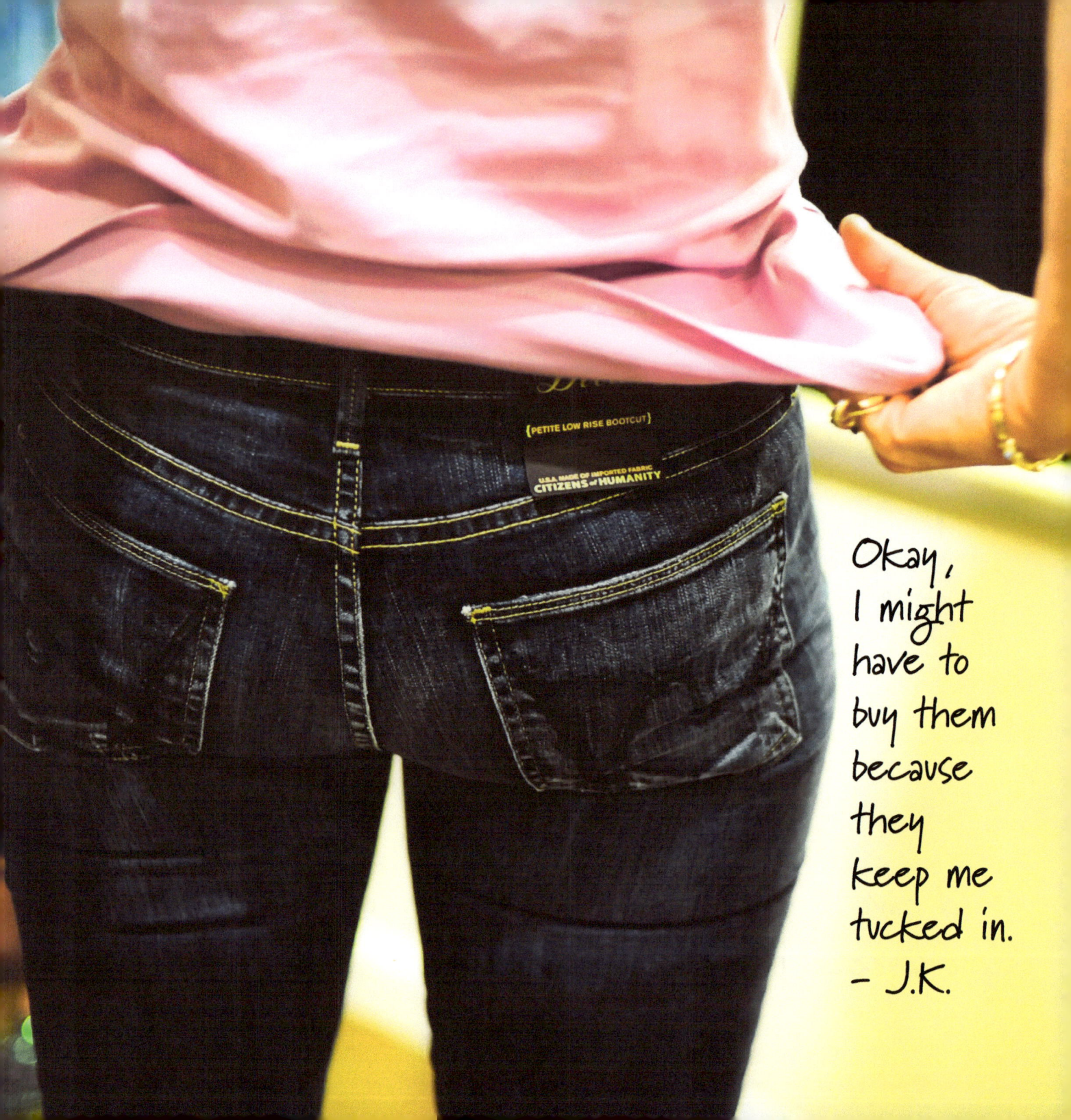

Okay, I might have to buy them because they keep me tucked in. - J.K.

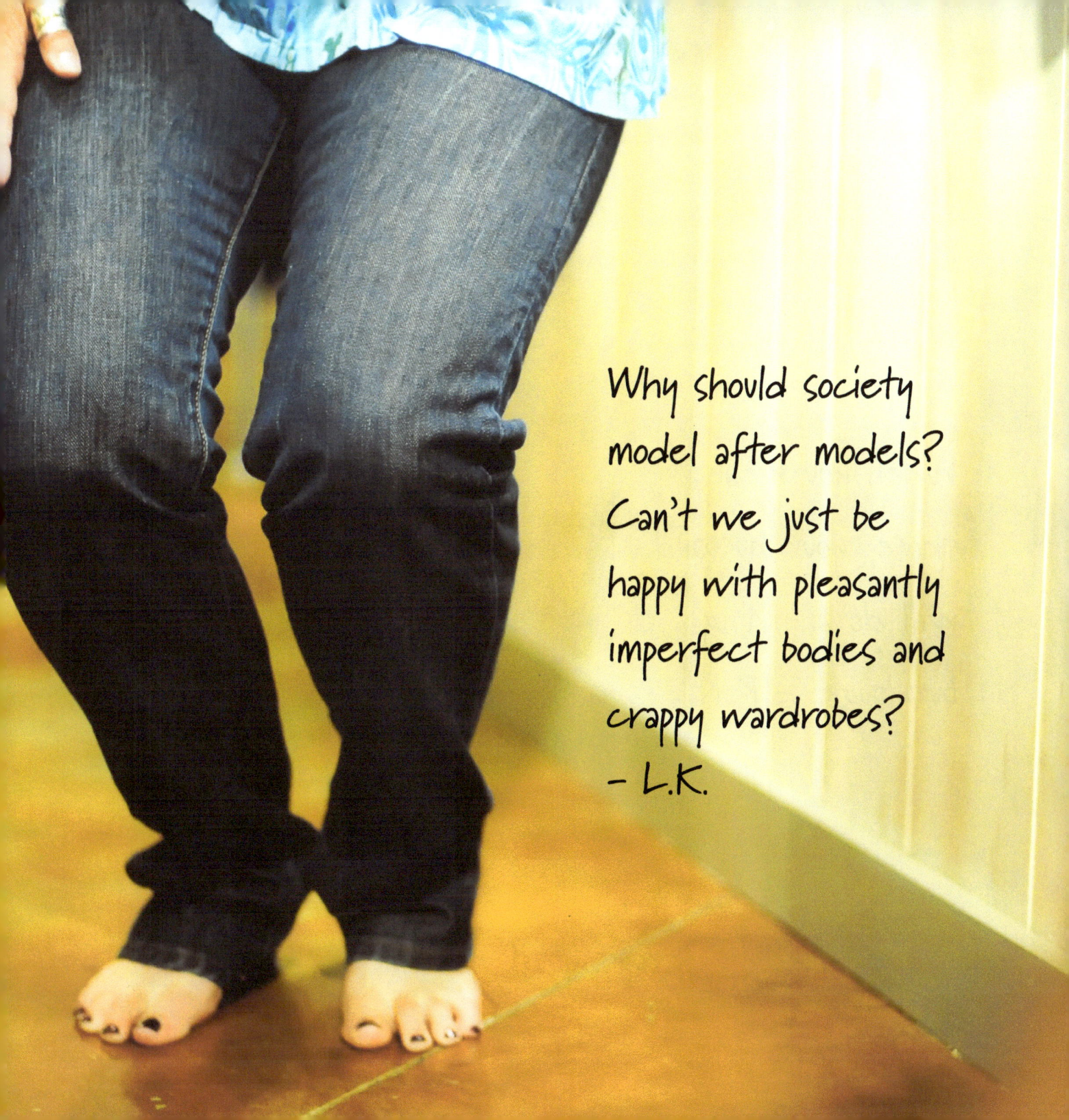

Why should society model after models? Can't we just be happy with pleasantly imperfect bodies and crappy wardrobes?
– L.K.

I like pockets on the ass. Pockets are sexy. – G.B.

When you wear those, your husband will do anything but laugh. – R.N.

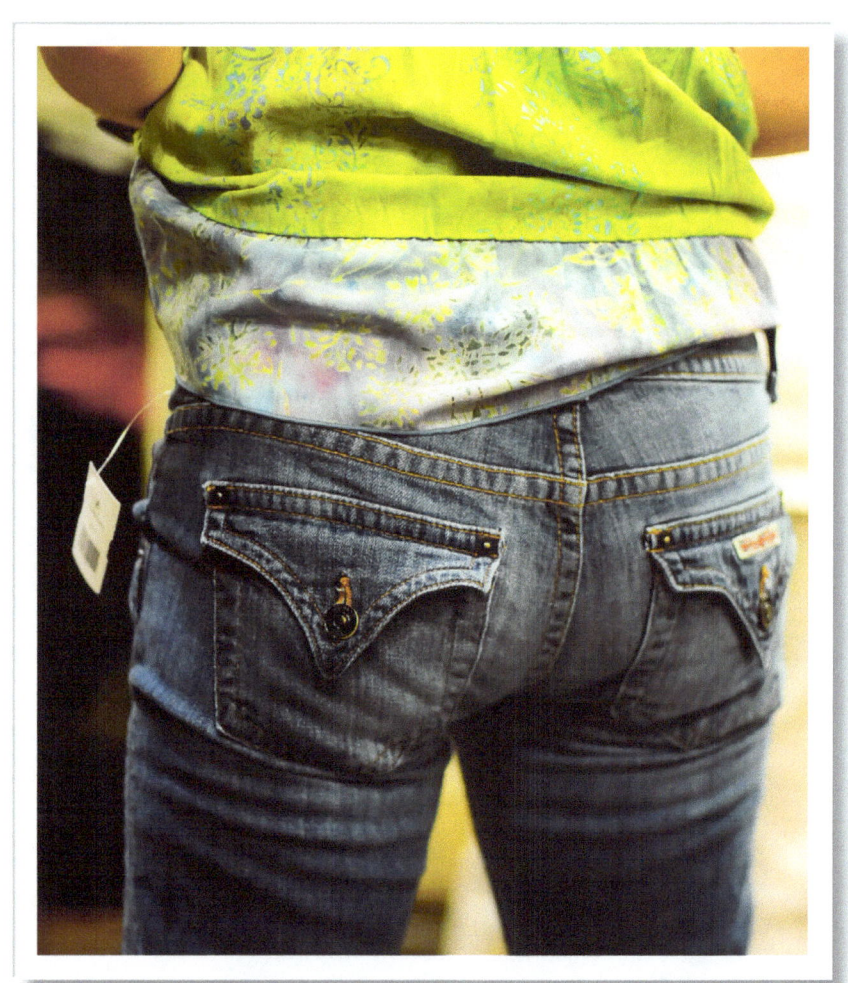

Do you mind if I grope you? – J.T.

Stilettos make every jean look hot! – H.A.

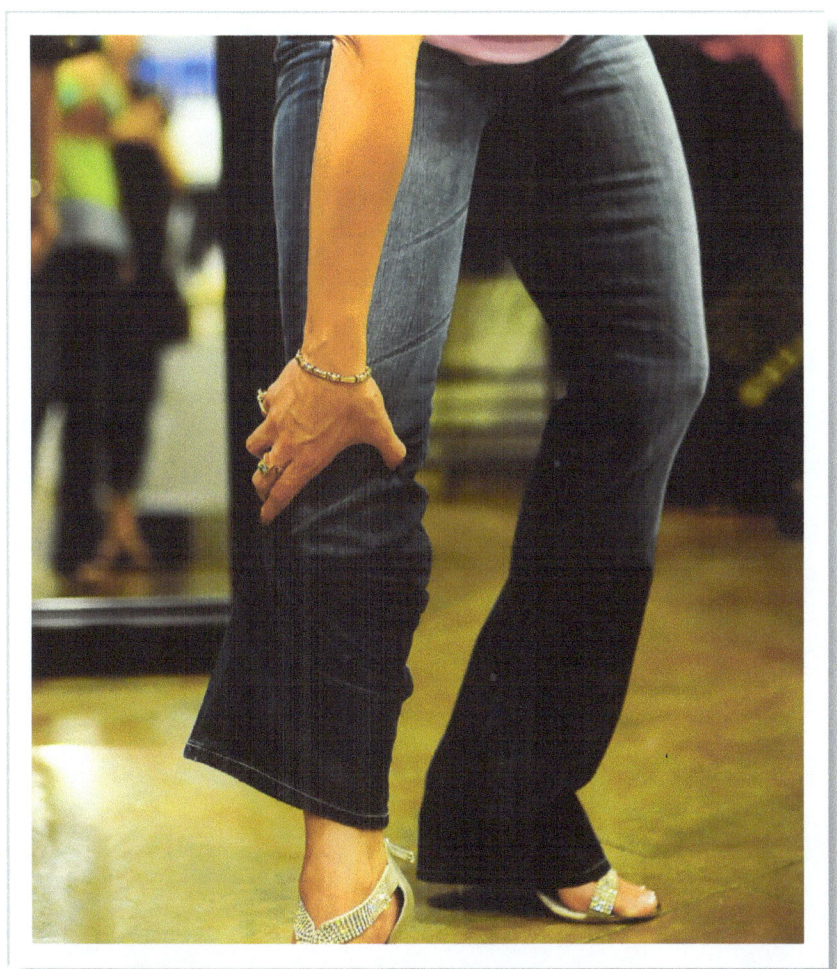

If these were on somebody else's body, they'd rock! – S.K.

I am completely poured into these jeans. – C.M.

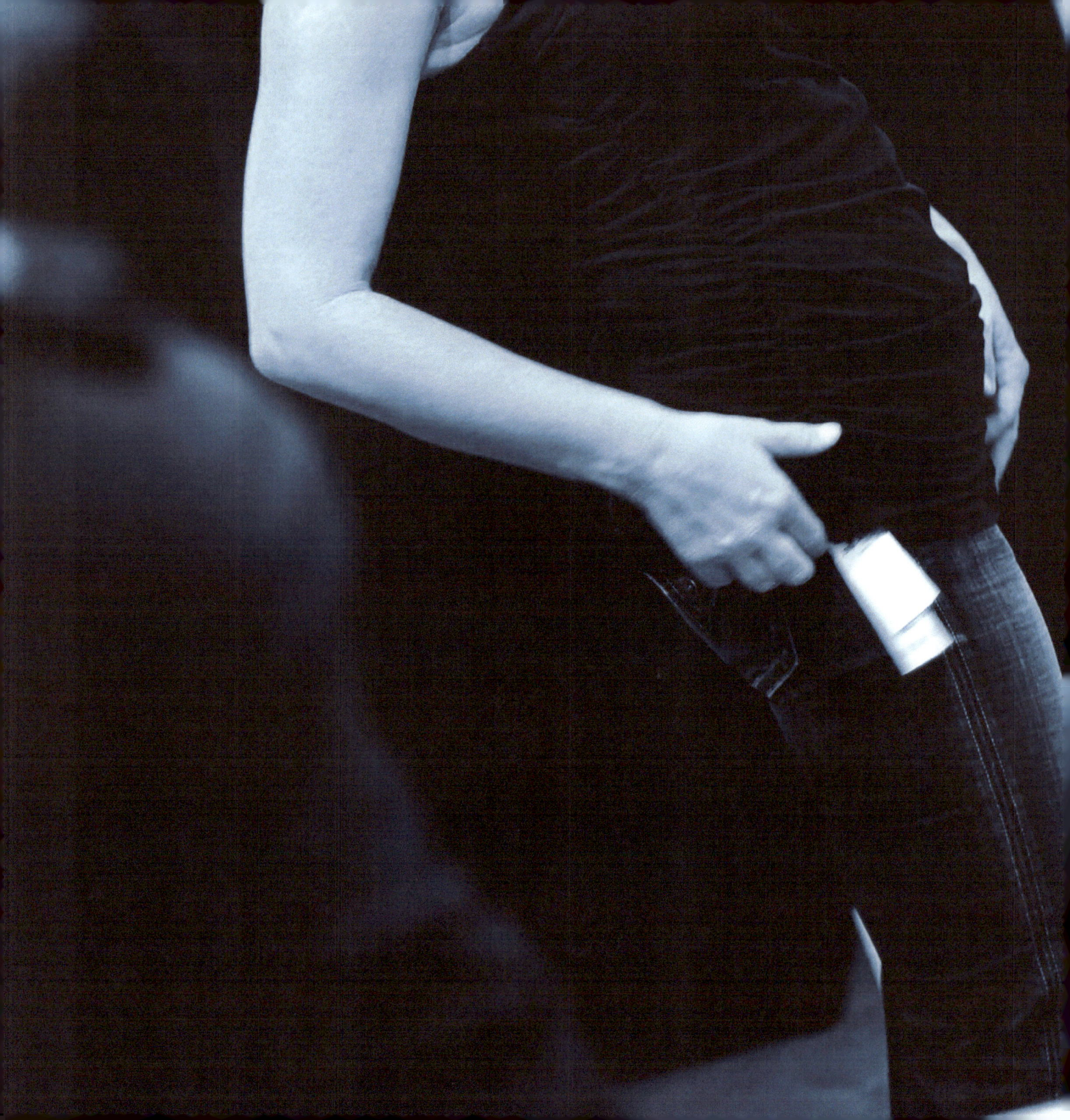

I think those jeans would be perfect for you if you just colored your hair, got a spray-on tan and did a quick 1,000 sit-ups. – Overheard

Do I wear a pair of low-rise that has a flop over or "Mom" jeans where I can tuck it in? – D.L.

I don't have muffin top, I have muffin thigh. – S.K.

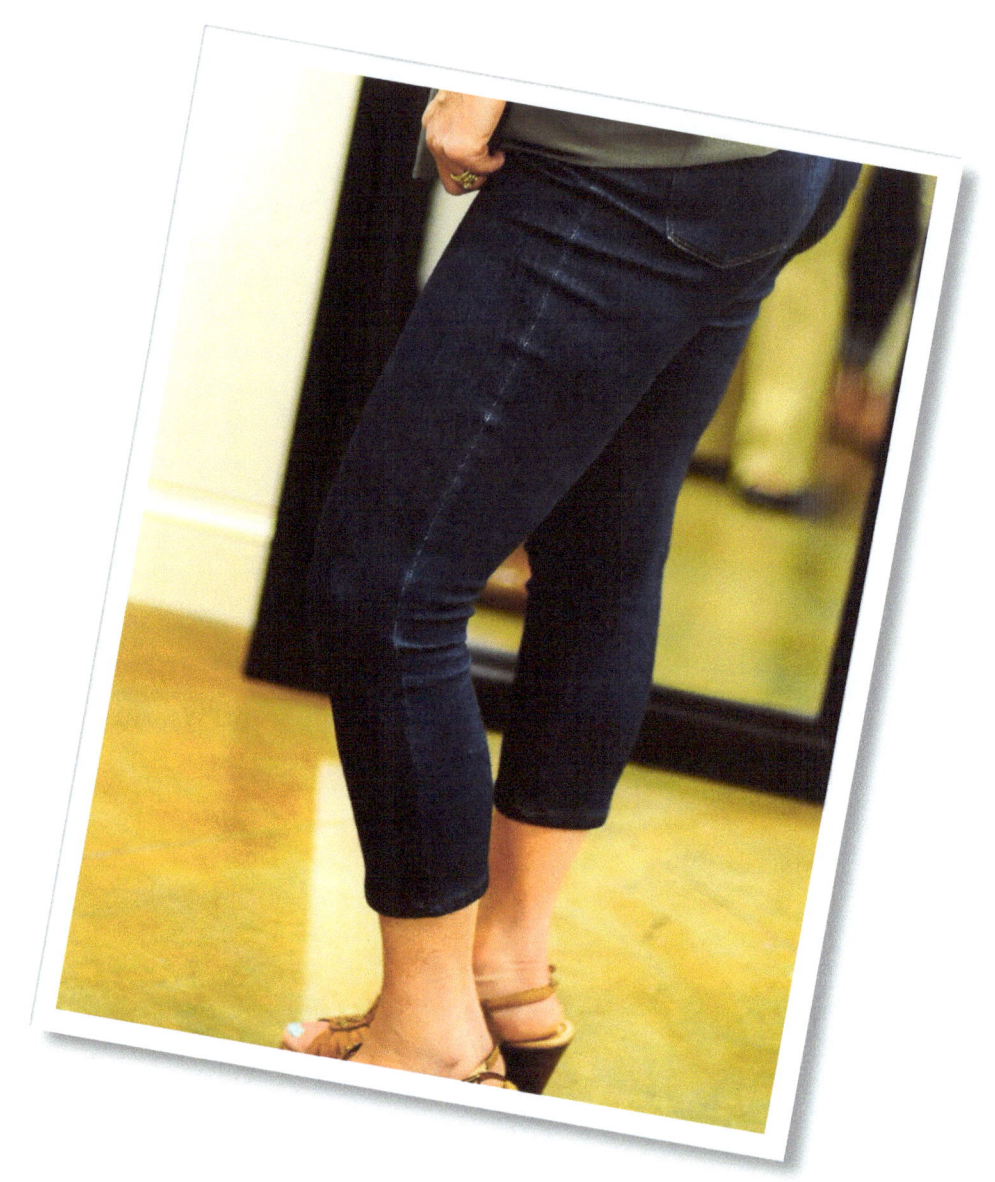

You would think after 1,000 million squats my butt would be cuter. - L.K.

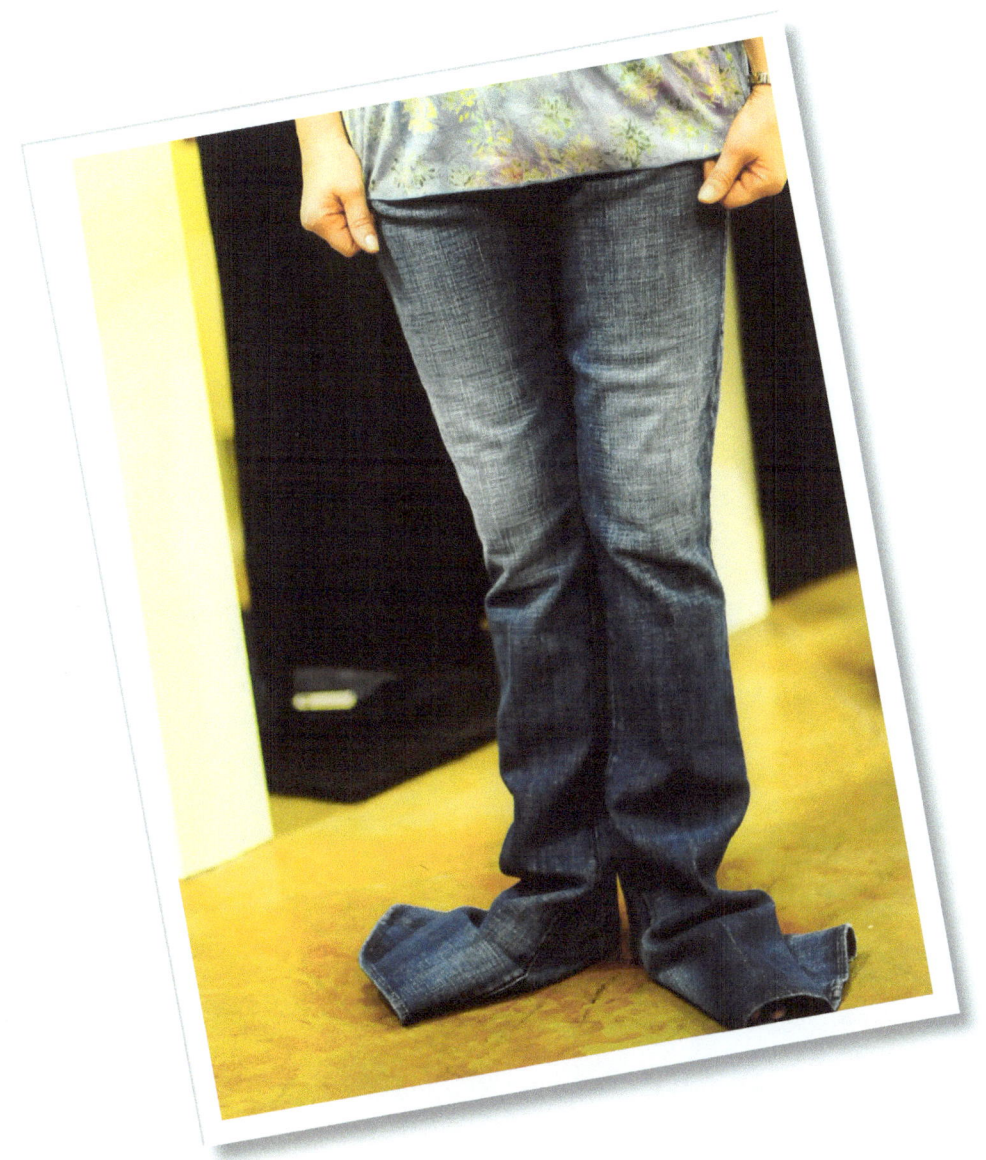

You can still wear your regular underwear in those.

– R.M.

How can jeans start ABOVE the pube line?
– Overheard

Why are these made so low? I have pulled
everything in and they still suck! – Overheard

Yes these jeans are expensive; but when Mommy's
happy, everybody's happy. – R.M.

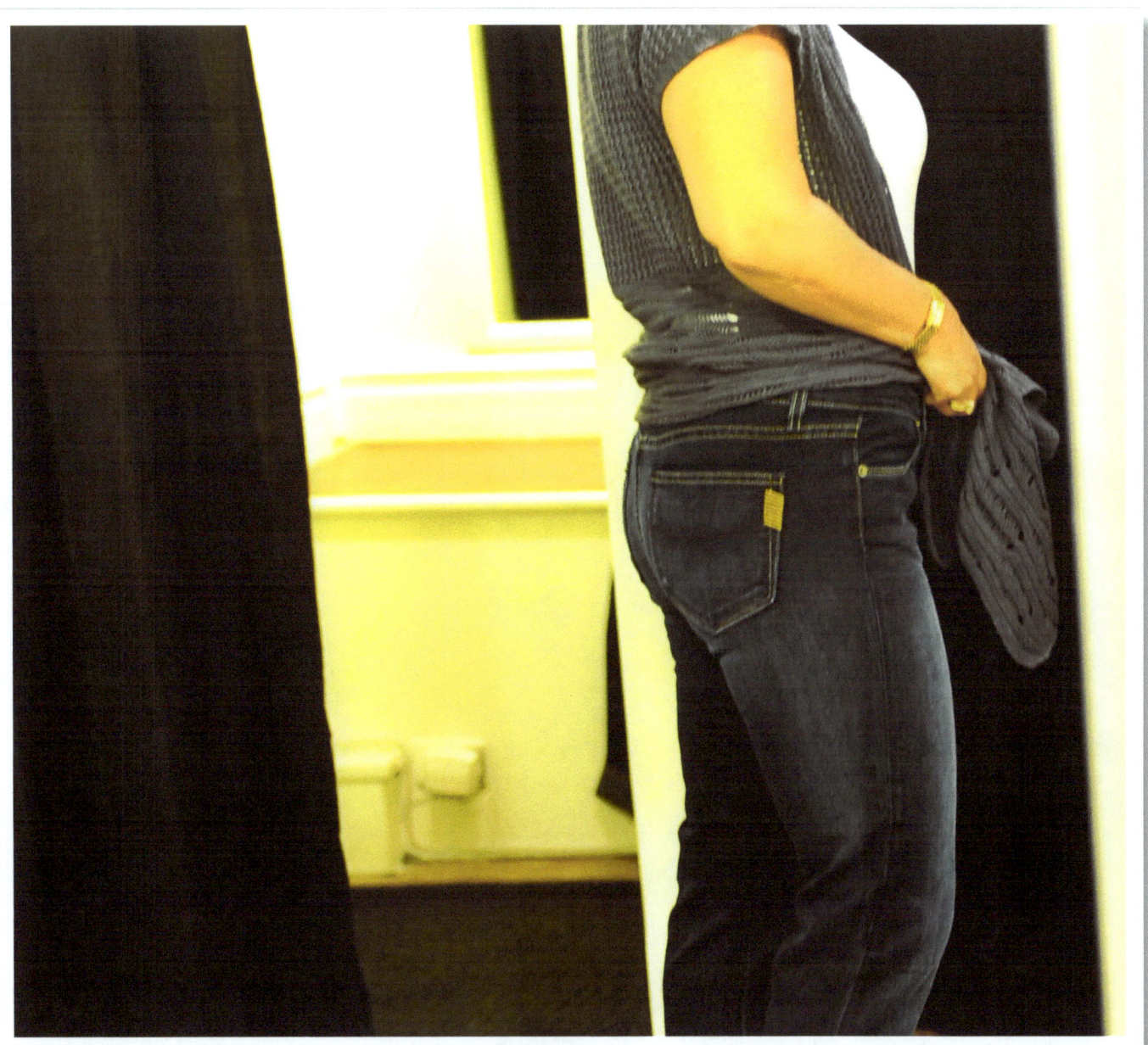

What idiot made this a real size? – D.L.

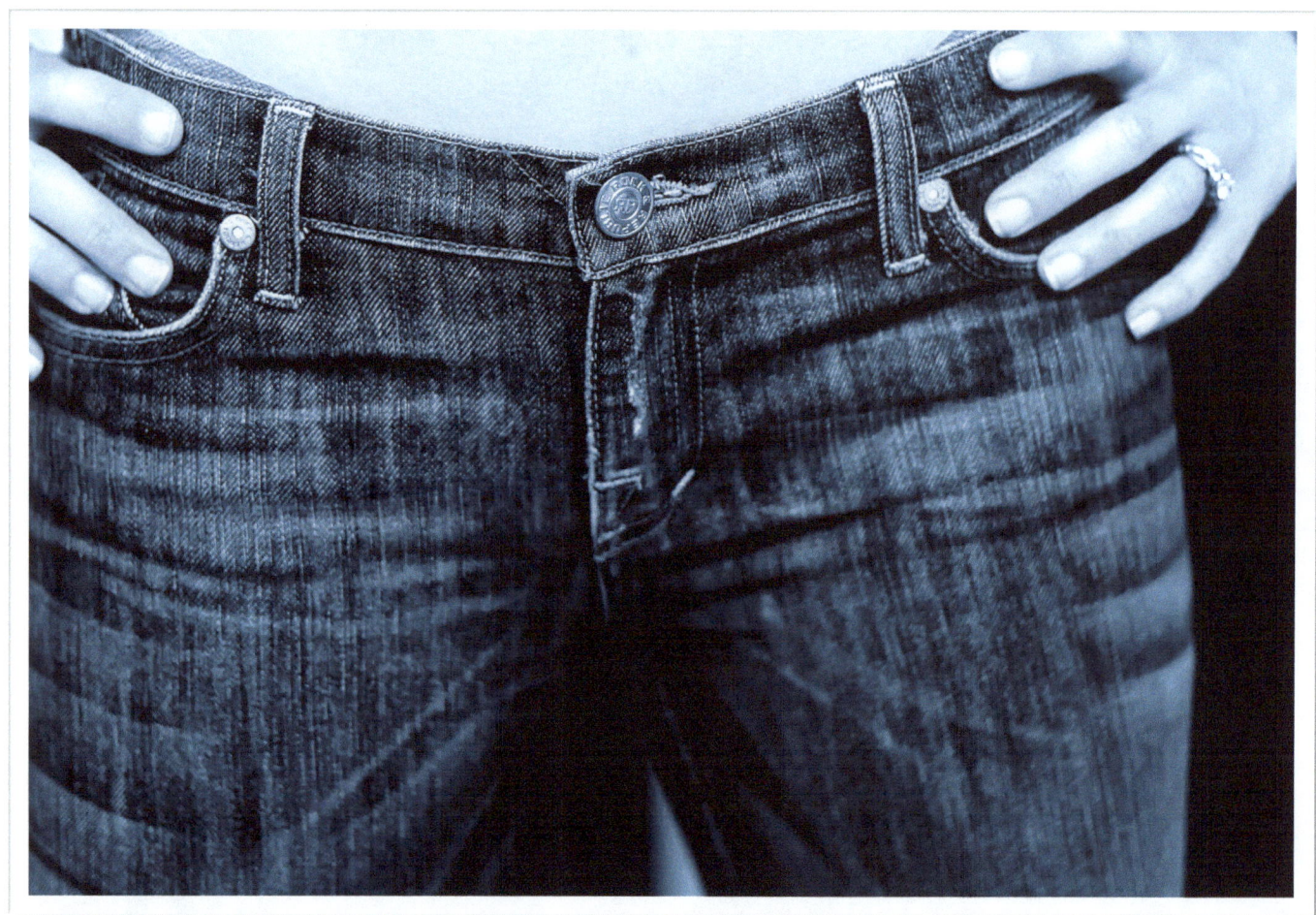

Hearing the phrase "great butt" pretty much forces me to purchase these jeans. – Overheard

An awesome pair of jeans is pointless unless it makes my husband want to peel them off me. – R.M.

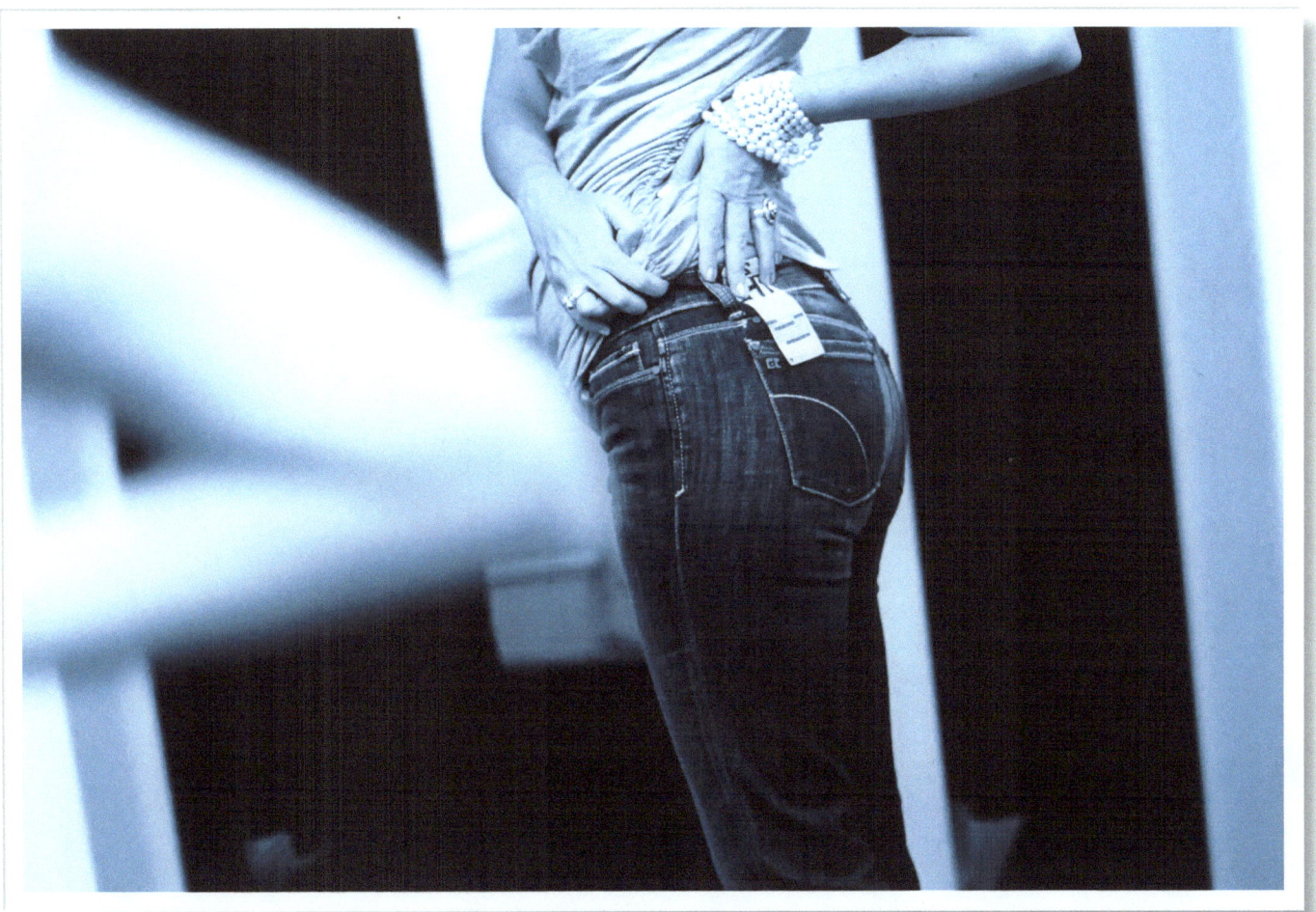

Wow! I'm potentially do-able in these sweet jeans!
– Overheard

Low-rise jeans aren't a trend you should be drawn towards; you should really have an aversion for them. They are a huge fashion no-no! – R.N.

I'm lumpy in all the wrong spots. – K.M.

Why do these make me look like I have two sets of boobs? – D.L.

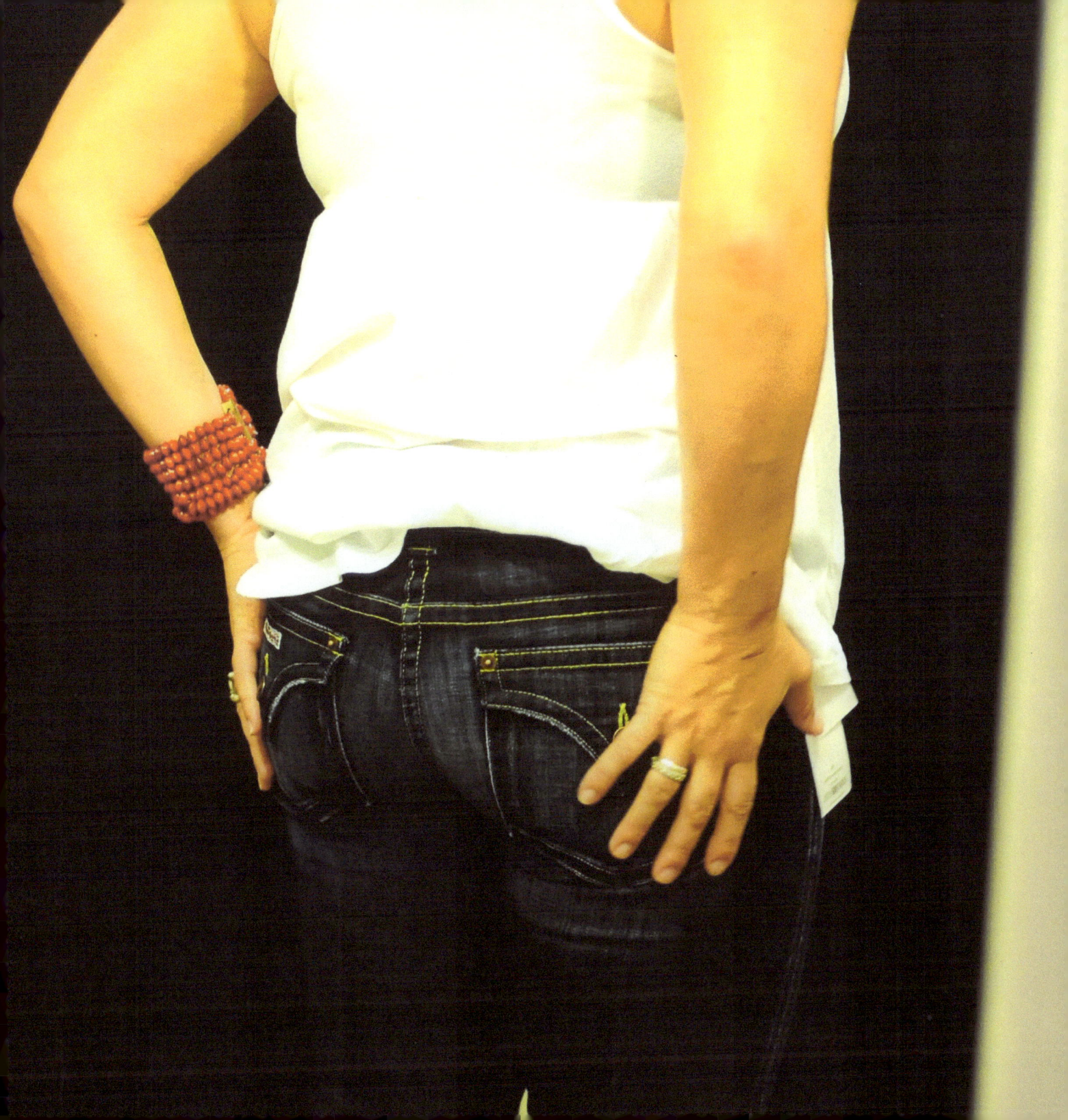

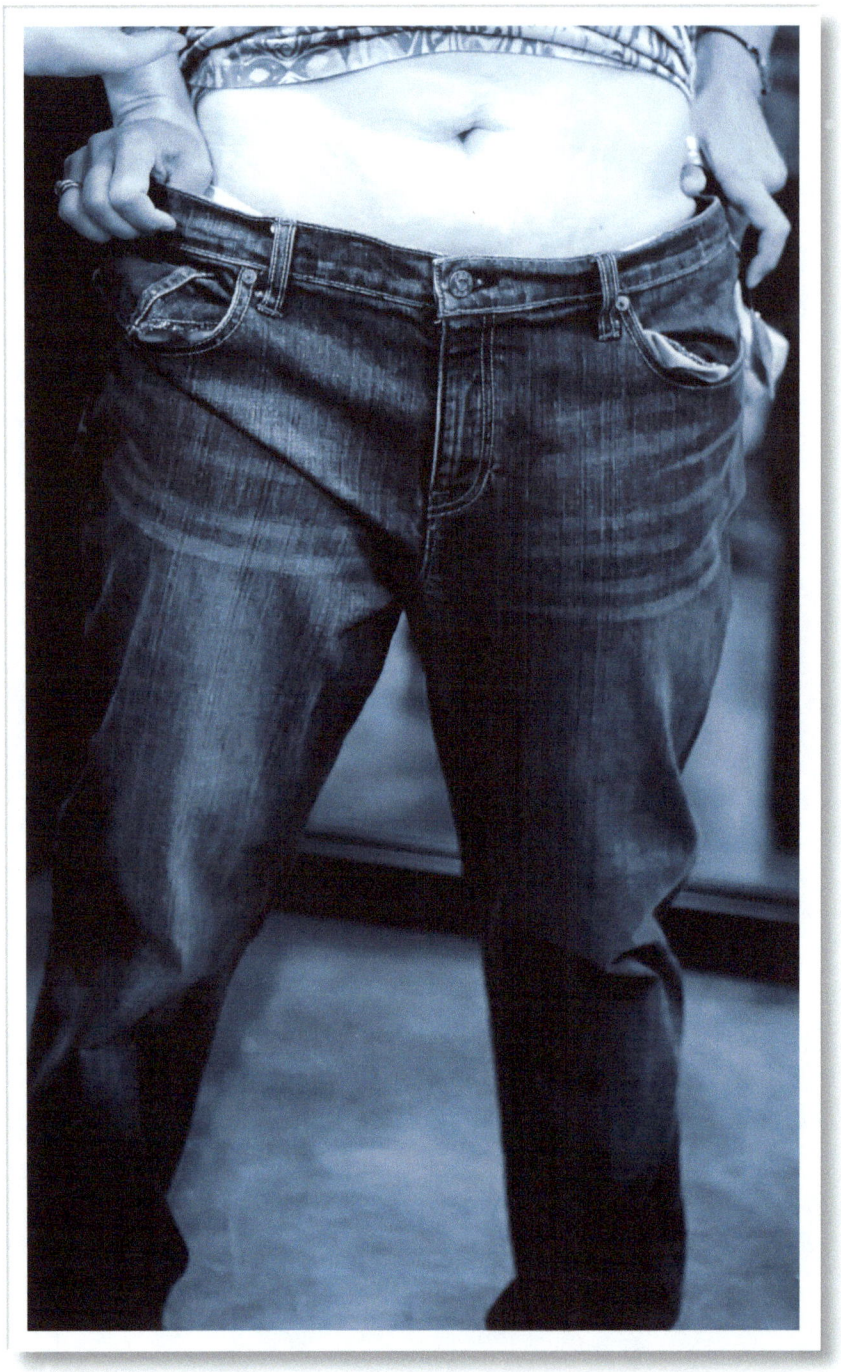

Lately, every pair of jeans has this nasty low-rise. Don't they know that it makes my muffin top bulge? – A.S.

Not on a good day! – S.N.

I'm stuffed in like a sausage and it's impossible to walk in these. – S.K.

They're good on my ass but not on my front. – K.R.

Wait, let me just throw up before trying on the next pair. – Overheard

These jeans are perfect right now. I haven't washed them in maybe 3 months. – G.B.

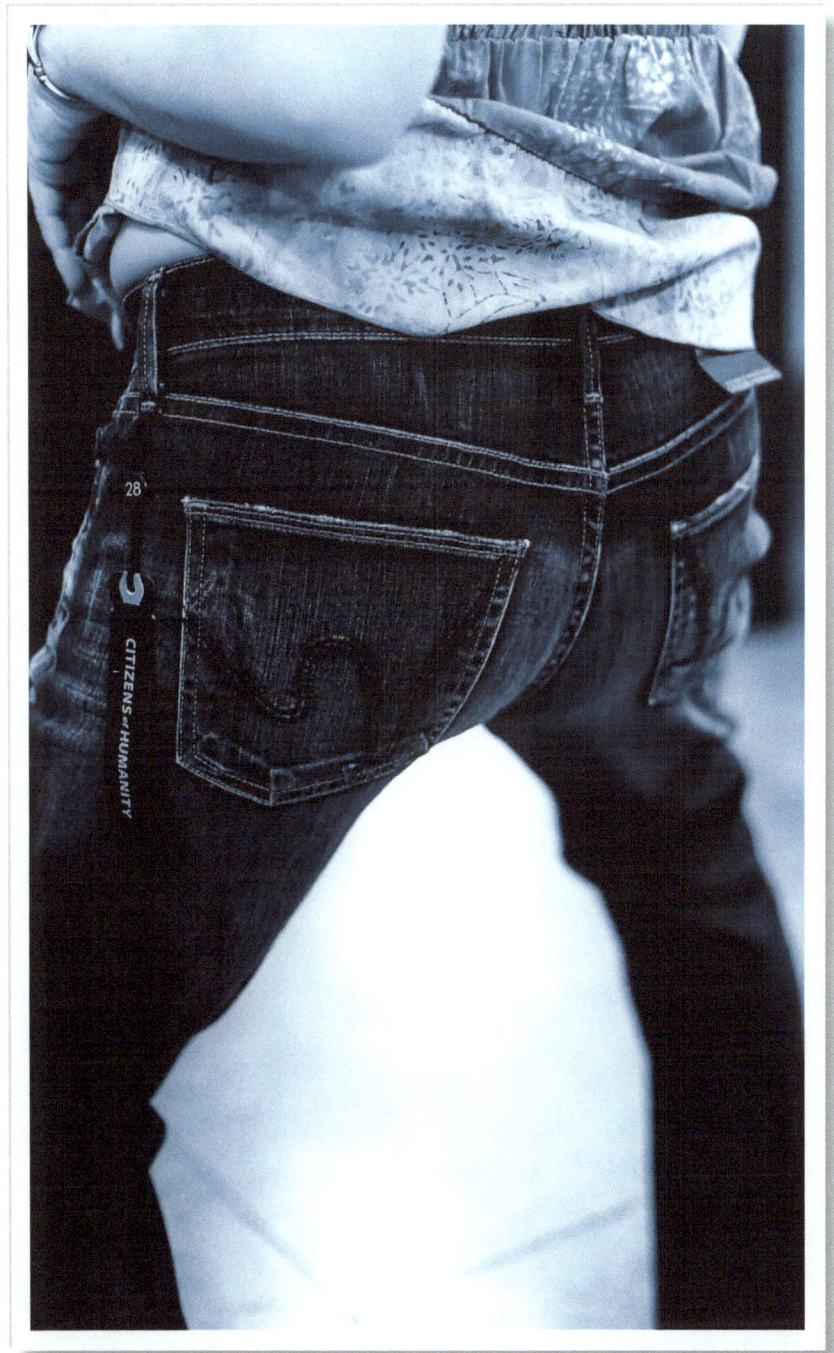

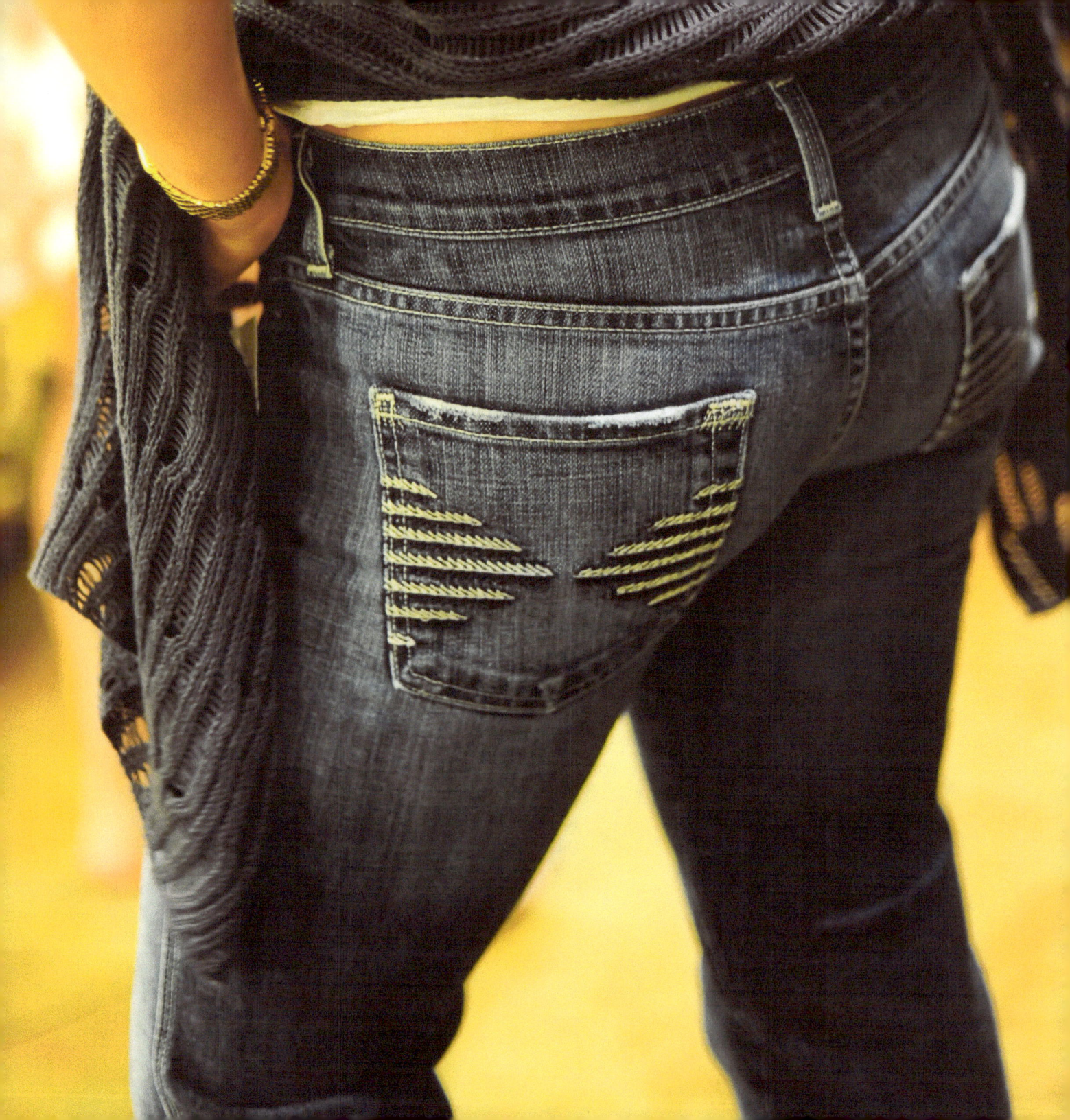

I don't think women should try on jeans unless they have just come from the gym, have recently fasted, or are really only twelve. – Overheard

If the jeans were hot enough, I would just not sit down. – R.M.

Wait, let me try them on again after I've had a pitcher of sangria. Maybe then I'll like them more. – L.K.

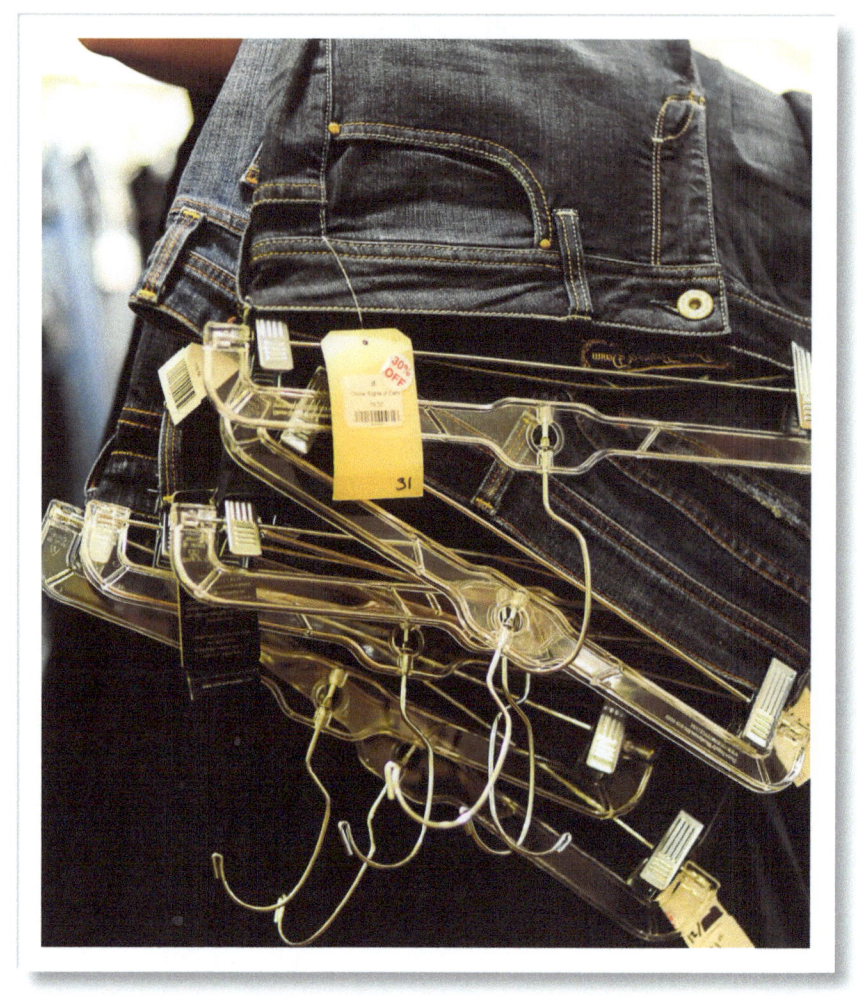

Now I have a front wedge. –A.C.

It is really HARD work getting skinny jeans off! – A.K.

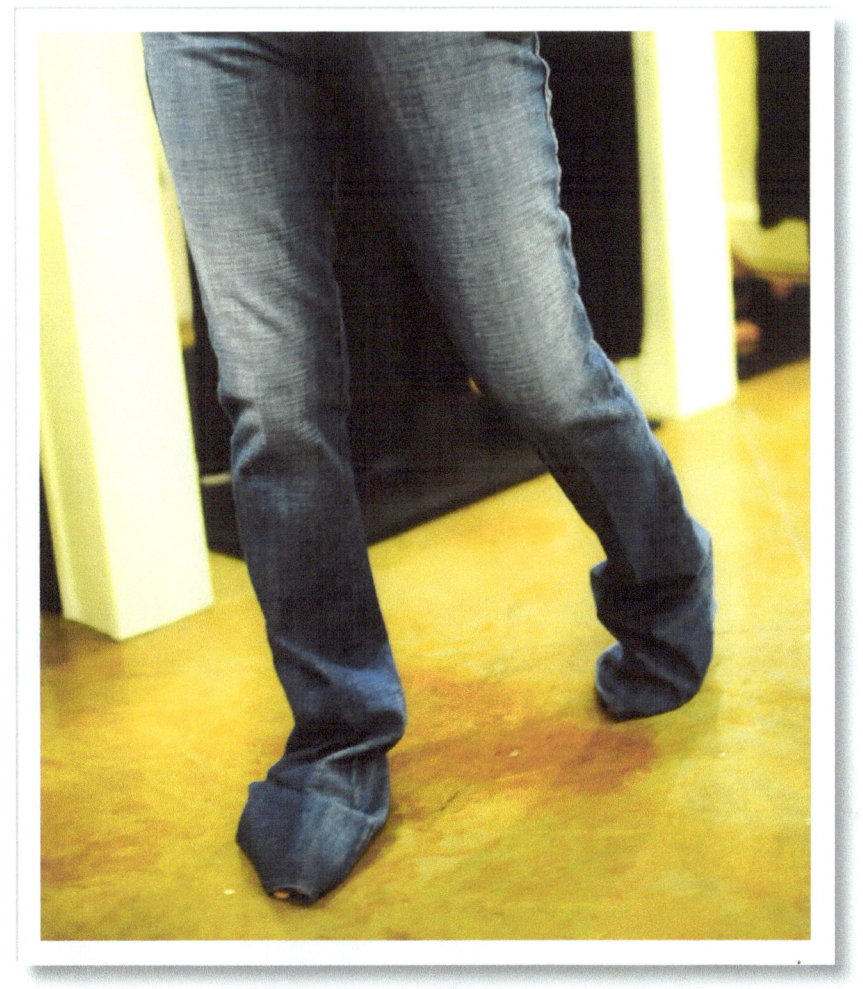

Who installed a fat mirror in here? – R.N.

I need to get that shit away from the top of my jeans.
– Overheard

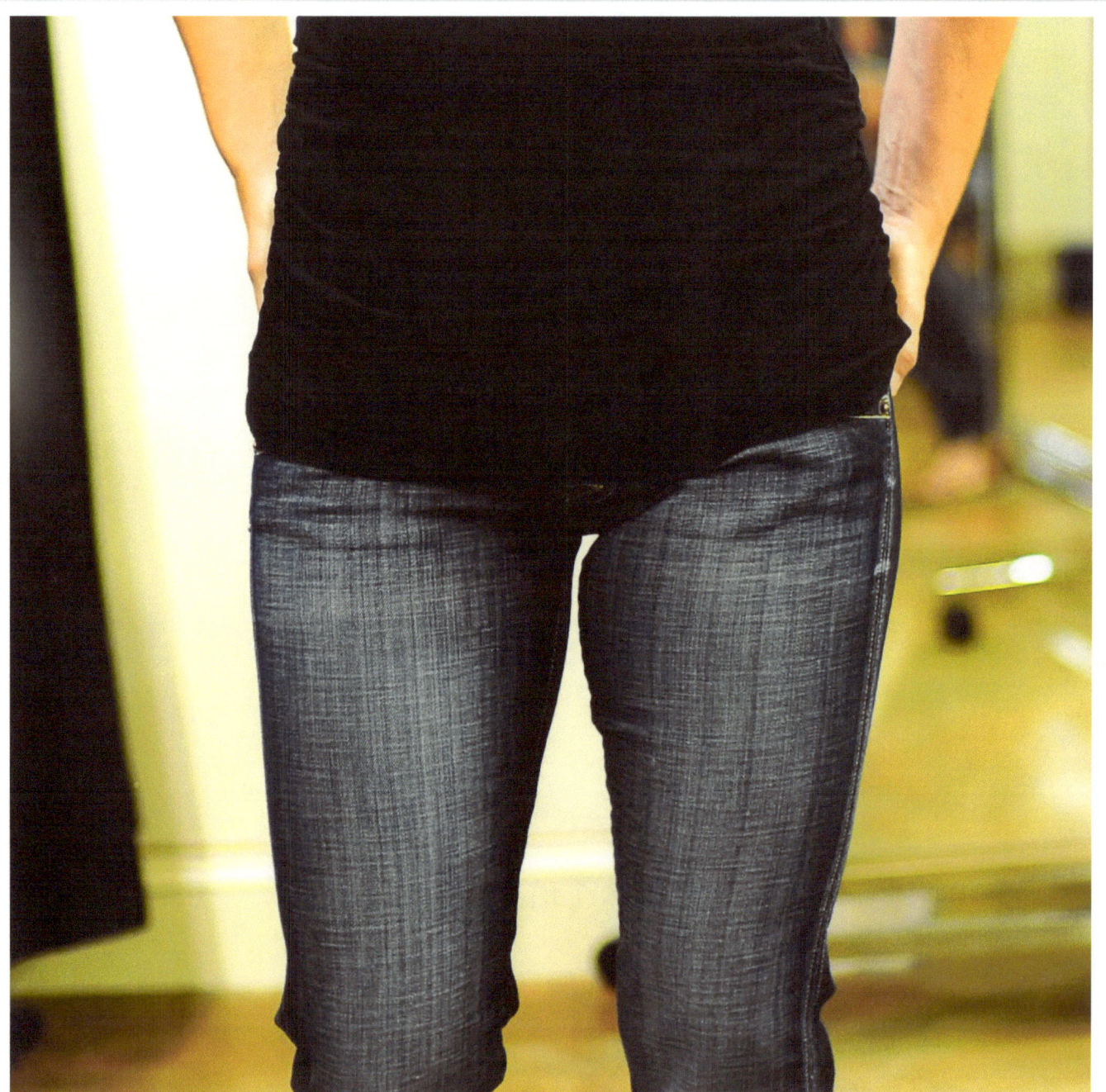

A pair of jeans can be your best friend
or it can really be a true bitch to you! – L.K.

About the Author

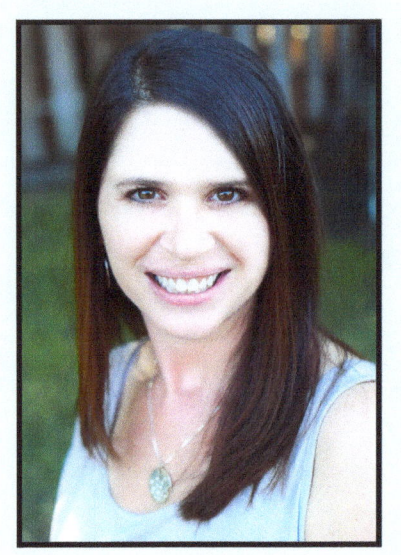

Lisa Katz grew up primarily in South Florida. She earned her Bachelor's degree in English from the University of Florida and continued her education to earn a Master's degree in Reading a couple of years later. In 1993, Lisa and her husband moved to Pittsburgh, PA where she worked as a Literacy Specialist. A few years down the road, she embraced her role as full-time mother. It was during this time that she began writing her first children's book. Lisa and her family moved to Charlottesville, Virginia and lived there for 10 years until recently settling into Gainesville, Florida in January 2012. Coming back to Gainesville after a 20-year hiatus has been a wonderful experience for Lisa. **Jean Expressions** is Lisa's debut women's book. She has written a feature-length screenplay as well as published a children's picture book, **The Little Boy Who Didn't Say "Bless You"**. Look for more women's books like this in the near future.